Git Magic

I0011451

Ben Lynn

Git Magic

Ben Lynn

Table of Contents

Preface

Git is a version control system initially designed and implemented by Linus Torvalds in 2005. Git quickly earned a place in my toolkit because it is fast, robust, flexible, simple, lightweight, scalable, and powerful.

However, Git has its drawbacks. In particular, it can bewilder beginners. When I started, I had to don safety gear: at the time, Git was so scary that I only ran it indirectly via a wrapper script named "cogito".

Happily, the situation improved rapidly and dramatically. The user interface underwent cosmetic surgery, making cogito obsolete. Volunteers worked hard on documentation, both official and unofficial. Books from reputable publishers materialized in the blink of an eye.

Too late for me. I had already learned Git's advanced features the hard way, namely through arduous trial and error. As I progressed, I kept notes on my website, "Git Magic". They proved unexpectedly popular: to my chagrin, far more popular than any code I've written. Thus I was motivated to maintain and update my website, which you're now reading in book form.

My website is freely accessible, along with its source: search for "git magic", install the **gitmagic** package on any Debian-based Linux distribution, or clone one of the following repositories:

- `git://repo.or.cz/gitmagic.git`

- `git://github.com/blynn/gitmagic.git`

- `git://gitorious.org/gitmagic/mainline.git`

(No idea what "clone" means? Then read this book!)

Perhaps you're wondering why I bothered with this quaint old-fashioned medium. It's all thanks to Carl Hu. In a gracious email, he suggested I convert my notes into a book: despite reading through a few books, he only truly appreciated Git when he found my website. As there may be others with a similar mindset, following his suggestion feels right.

This book is not meant to be a reference. There are help pages for that, as well as the user manual. And the source code! Instead, we approach Git as I once did: as a lazy programmer who just wants to get stuff done. For each task, we try to teach as little Git as possible, though by the end, you can't help but develop a good understanding of this amazing tool.

I'm flattered that others have taken the trouble to translate my website. Thanks to JunJie, Meng and JiangWei for the Simplified Chinese translation (I hope to learn your full names one day so I can acknowledge you properly), Rodrigo Toledo for the Spanish translation, and Leonardo Siqueira Rodrigues for the Portuguese translation.

Thanks also to Daniel Baumann and François Marier for maintaining the Debian package, as well as Dustin Sallings, Alberto Bertogli, James Cameron, Douglas Livingstone, Michael Budde, Richard Albury, Tarmigan, Derek Mahar, Frode Aannevik, Keith Rarick, Andy Somerville, Ralf Recker, Øyvind A. Holm, Miklos Vajna, Sébastien Hinderer, Thomas Miedema, and Joe Malin for suggestions, corrections and improvements.

Lastly, my gratitude goes to many others for your support and praise. I considered quoting some of you on the back cover to promote this book, but your words might raise expectations to ridiculous heights!

Chapter 1. Introduction

I've played video games almost all my life. In contrast, I only started using version control systems as an adult. I suspect I'm not alone, and comparing the two may make these concepts easier to explain and understand.

Think of editing your code, or document, as playing a game. Once you've made a lot of progress, you click on the *Save* button in your trusty editor to keep your work.

But this will overwrite the previous version. It's like those old school games which only had one save slot: sure you could save, but you could never go back to an older state. Which was a shame, because your previous save might have been right at an exceptionally fun part of the game that you'd like to revisit one day. Or worse still, your current save is in an unwinnable state, and you have to start again.

1.1. Version control

When editing, you can *Save As...* a different file, or copy the file somewhere first before saving if you want to savour old versions. You can compress them too to save space. This is a primitive and labour-intensive form of version control. Computer games improved on this long ago, many of them providing multiple automatically timestamped save slots.

Let's make the problem slightly tougher. Say you have a bunch of files that go together, such as source code for a project, or files for a website. Now if you want to keep an old version you have to archive a whole directory. Keeping many versions around by hand is inconvenient, and quickly becomes expensive.

With some computer games, a saved game really does consist of a directory full of files. These games hide this detail from the player and present a convenient interface to manage various versions of this directory.

Version control systems are no different. They all have nice interfaces to manage a directory of stuff. You can save the state of the directory every so often, and you can load any one of the saved states later on. Unlike most computer games, they're usually smart about conserving space. Typically, only a few files change between version to version, and not by much. Storing the differences instead of entire new copies saves room.

1.2. Distributed version control

Now imagine a very difficult computer game. So difficult to finish that many experienced gamers all over the world decide to team up and share their saved games to try to beat it. Speedruns are real-life examples: players specializing in different levels of the same game collaborate to produce amazing results.

How would you set up a system so they can get at each other's saves easily? And upload new ones?

In the old days, every project used centralized version control. A server somewhere held all the saved games. Nobody else did. Every player kept at most a few saved games on their machine. When a player wanted to make progress, they'd download the latest save from the main server, play a while, save and upload back to the server for everyone else to use.

What if a player wanted to get an older saved game for some reason? Maybe the current saved game is in an unwinnable state because somebody forgot to pick up an object back in level three, and they want to find the latest saved game where the game can still be completed. Or maybe they want to compare two older saved games to see how much work a particular player did.

There could be many reasons to want to see an older revision, but the outcome is the same. They have to ask the central server for that old saved game. The more saved games they want, the more they need to communicate.

The new generation of version control systems, of which Git is a member, are known as distributed systems, and can be thought of as a generalization of centralized systems. When players download from the main server they get every saved game, not just the latest one. It's as if they're mirroring the central server.

This initial cloning operation can be expensive, especially if there's a long history, but it pays off in the long run. One immediate benefit is that when an old save is desired for any reason, communication with the central server is unnecessary.

1.3. Distribution is not anarchy

A popular misconception is that distributed systems are ill-suited for projects requiring an official central repository. Nothing could be further from the truth. Photographing someone does not cause their soul to be stolen. Similarly, cloning the master repository does not diminish its importance.

A good first approximation is that anything a centralized version control system can do, a well-designed distributed system can do better. Network resources are simply costlier than local resources. While there are drawbacks to a distributed approach, one is less likely to make erroneous comparisons with this rule of thumb.

A small project may only need a fraction of the features offered by such a system, but using systems that scale poorly for tiny projects is like using Roman numerals for calculations involving small numbers.

Moreover, your project may grow beyond your original expectations. Using Git from the outset is like carrying a Swiss army knife even though you mostly use it to open bottles. On the day you desperately need a screwdriver you'll be glad you have more than a plain bottle-opener.

1.4. Merge conflicts

For this topic, our computer game analogy becomes too thinly stretched. Instead, let us again consider editing a document.

Suppose Alice inserts a line at the beginning of a file, and Bob appends one at the end of his copy. They both upload their changes. Most systems will automatically deduce a reasonable course of action: accept and merge their changes, so both Alice's and Bob's edits are applied.

Now suppose both Alice and Bob have made distinct edits to the same line. Then it is impossible to proceed without human intervention. The second person to upload is informed of a *merge conflict*, and must choose one edit over another, or revise the line entirely:

```
The most hardcore programmers write their own text editors,
expending inordinate amounts of time and effort. Fortunately,
the rest of us can choose from a myriad of free high-quality
offerings. But first, a safety warning about the worst text
editor ever:

<<<<<<< alice:example.txt
Avoid Emacs at all cost. Some joke that Emacs is a great
operating system, lacking only a decent editor. Actually,
this is not far from the truth: Emacs is a bloated abomination
that grudgingly allows the user to edit text.
=======
Whatever you do, never edit with vi. Its interface dates from
the Stone Age. Actually, even before the Stone Age they probably
had better interfaces: even nuanced grunts are more expressive
than the cryptic beeps that accompany every keystroke.
>>>>>>> bob:example.txt

Unpleasantries aside, let us now turn our attention to reasonable
text editors.
```

More complex situations can arise. Version control systems handle the simpler cases themselves, and leave the difficult cases for humans. Usually their behaviour is configurable.

Chapter 2. Basics

Rather than diving into a sea of Git commands, use these elementary examples to get your feet wet. Despite their simplicity, each of them are useful. Indeed, in my first months with Git I never ventured beyond these shallow waters.

2.1. Saving state

About to attempt something drastic? Before you do, take a snapshot of all files in the current directory with:

```
$ git init
$ git add .
$ git commit -m "My first backup"
```

Now if your new edits go awry, restore the pristine version:

```
$ git reset --hard
```

To save the state again:

```
$ git commit -a -m "Another backup"
```

2.2. Add, delete, rename

The above only keeps track of the files that were present when you first ran **git add**. If you add new files or subdirectories, you'll have to tell Git:

```
$ git add readme.txt Documentation
```

Similarly, if you want Git to forget about certain files:

```
$ git rm kludge.h obsolete.c
$ git rm -r incriminating/evidence/
```

Git deletes these files for you if you haven't already.

Renaming a file is the same as removing the old name and adding the new name. There's also the shortcut **git mv** which has the same syntax as the **mv** command. For example:

```
$ git mv bug.c feature.c
```

2.3. Advanced undo/redo

Sometimes you just want to go back and forget about every change past a certain point because they're all wrong. Then:

```
$ git log
```

shows you a list of recent commits, and their SHA1 hashes:

```
commit 766f9881690d240ba334153047649b8b8f11c664
Author: Bob <bob@example.com>
Date:   Tue Mar 14 01:59:26 2000 -0800

    Replace printf() with write().

commit 82f5ea346a2e651544956a8653c0f58dc151275c
Author: Alice <alice@example.com>
Date:   Thu Jan 1 00:00:00 1970 +0000

    Initial commit.
```

The first few characters of the hash are enough to specify the commit; alternatively, copy and paste the entire hash. Type:

```
$ git reset --hard 766f
```

to restore the state to a given commit and erase all newer commits from the record permanently.

Other times you want to hop to an old state briefly. In this case, type:

```
$ git checkout 82f5
```

This takes you back in time, while preserving newer commits. However, like time travel in a science-fiction movie, if you now edit and commit, you will be in an alternate reality, because your actions are different to what they were the first time around.

This alternate reality is called a *branch*, and we'll have more to say about this later. For now, just remember that

```
$ git checkout master
```

will take you back to the present. Also, to stop Git complaining, always commit or reset your changes before running checkout.

To take the computer game analogy again:

- **git reset --hard**: load an old save and delete all saved games newer than the one just loaded.

- **git checkout**: load an old game, but if you play on, the game state will deviate from the newer saves you made the first time around. Any saved games you make now will end up in a separate branch representing the alternate reality you have entered. We deal with this later.

You can choose only to restore particular files and subdirectories by appending them after the command:

```
$ git checkout 82f5 some.file another.file
```

Take care, as this form of **checkout** can silently overwrite files. To prevent accidents, commit before running any checkout command, especially when first learning Git. In general, whenever you feel unsure about any operation, Git command or not, first run **git commit -a**.

Don't like cutting and pasting hashes? Then use:

```
$ git checkout :/"My first b"
```

to jump to the commit that starts with a given message. You can also ask for the 5th-last saved state:

```
$ git checkout master~5
```

2.4. Reverting

In a court of law, events can be stricken from the record. Likewise, you can pick specific commits to undo:

```
$ git commit -a
$ git revert 1b6d
```

will undo just the commit with the given hash. The revert is recorded as a new commit, which you can confirm by running **git log**.

2.5. Changelog generation

Generate a changelog by typing:

```
$ git log > ChangeLog
```

2.6. Downloading a project

Get a copy of a project managed with Git by typing:

```
$ git clone git://server/path/to/files
```

For example, to get all the files I used to create this site:

```
$ git clone git://git.or.cz/gitmagic.git
```

We'll have much to say about the **clone** command soon.

2.7. The bleeding edge

If you've already downloaded a copy of a project using **git clone**, you can upgrade to the latest version with:

```
$ git pull
```

2.8. Instant publishing

Suppose you've written a script you'd like to share with others. You could just tell them to download from your computer, but if they do so while you're improving the script or making experimental changes, they could wind up in trouble. Of course, this is why release cycles exist. Developers may work on a project frequently, but they only make the code available when they feel it is presentable.

To do this with Git, in the directory where your script resides:

```
$ git init
$ git add .
$ git commit -m "First release"
```

Then tell your users to run:

```
$ git clone your.computer:/path/to/script
```

to download your script. This assumes they have ssh access. If not, run **git daemon** and tell your users to instead run:

```
$ git clone git://your.computer/path/to/script
```

From now on, every time your script is ready for release, execute:

```
$ git commit -a -m "Next release"
```

and your users can upgrade their version by changing to the directory containing your script and typing:

```
$ git pull
```

Your users will never end up with a version of your script you don't want them to see.

2.9. What have I done?

Find out what changes you've made since the last commit with:

```
$ git diff
```

Or since yesterday:

```
$ git diff "@{yesterday}"
```

Or between a particular version and 2 versions ago:

```
$ git diff 1b6d "master~2"
```

In each case the output is a patch that can be applied with **git apply**. Try also:

```
$ git whatchanged --since="2 weeks ago"
```

Often I'll browse history with **qgit** instead, due to its slick photogenic interface, or **tig**, a text-mode interface that works well over slow connections. Alternatively, install a web server, run **git instaweb** and fire up any web browser.

2.10. Exercise

Let A, B, C, D be four successive commits where B is the same as A except some files have been removed. We want to add the files back at D. How can we do this?

There are at least three solutions. Assuming we are at D:

1. The difference between A and B are the removed files. We can create a patch representing this difference and apply it:

   ```
   $ git diff B A | git apply
   ```

2. Since we saved the files back at A, we can retrieve them:

   ```
   $ git checkout A foo.c bar.h
   ```

3. We can view going from A to B as a change we want to undo:

   ```
   $ git revert B
   ```

Which choice is best? Whichever you prefer most. It is easy to get what you want with Git, and often there are many ways to get it.

Chapter 3. Clones

In older version control systems, checkout is the standard operation to get files. You retrieve a bunch of files in a particular saved state.

In Git and other distributed version control systems, cloning is the standard operation. To get files, you create a *clone* of the entire repository. In other words, you practically mirror the central server. Anything the main repository can do, you can do.

3.1. Staying in sync

I can tolerate making tarballs or using **rsync** for backups and basic syncing. But sometimes I edit on my laptop, other times on my desktop, and the two may not have talked to each other in between.

Initialize a Git repository and commit your files on one machine. Then on the other:

```
$ git clone other.computer:/path/to/files
```

to create a second copy of the files and Git repository. From now on,

```
$ git commit -a
$ git pull other.computer:/path/to/files HEAD
```

will *pull* in the state of the files on the other computer into the one you're working on. If you've recently made conflicting edits in the same file, Git will let you know and you should commit again after resolving them.

Think of HEAD as a cursor that points at the latest commit and advances with each new commit. Several commands take HEAD as the default argument, and until now, we have never needed to explicitly specify it. In the above pull, it refers to the latest commit on the other computer.

3.2. Classic source control

Initialize a Git repository for your files:

```
$ git init
$ git add .
$ git commit -m "Initial commit"
```

On the central server, initialize a *bare repository* in some directory:

```
$ mkdir proj.git
$ cd proj.git
$ git init --bare
$  # one-line variant: GIT_DIR=proj.git git init
```

Start the Git daemon if necessary:

```
$ git daemon --detach  # it may already be running
```

For Git hosting services, follow the instructions to setup the initially empty Git repository. Typically one fills in a form on a webpage.

Push your project to the central server with:

```
$ git push git://central.server/path/to/proj.git HEAD
```

To check out the source, a developer types:

```
$ git clone git://central.server/path/to/proj.git
```

After making changes, the developer saves changes locally:

```
$ git commit -a
```

To update to the latest version:

```
$ git pull
```

Any merge conflicts should be resolved then committed:

```
$ git commit -a
```

To check in local changes into the central repository:

```
$ git push
```

If the main server has new changes due to activity by other developers, the push fails, and the developer should pull the latest version, resolve any merge conflicts, then try again.

3.3. Bare repositories

A bare repository is so named because it has no working directory;
it only contains files that are normally hidden away in the .git
subdirectory. In other words, it maintains the history of a project,
and never holds a snapshot of any given version.

A bare repository plays a role similar to that of the main server
in a centralized version control system: the home of your project.
Developers clone your project from it, and push the latest official
changes to it. Typically it resides on a server that does little else but
disseminate data. Development occurs in the clones, so the home
repository can do without a working directory.

Many Git commands fail on bare repositories unless the GIT_DIR
environment variable is set to the repository path, or the --bare
option is supplied.

3.4. Push versus pull

 Why did we introduce the push command, rather than rely on the
familiar pull command? Firstly, pulling fails on bare repositories:
instead you must *fetch*, a command we later discuss. But even if we
kept a normal repository on the central server, pulling into it would
still be cumbersome. We would have to login to the server first, and
give the pull command the network address of the machine we're
pulling from. Firewalls may interfere, and what if we have no shell
access to the server in the first place?

However, apart from this case, we discourage pushing into a
repository, because confusion can ensue when the destination has a
working directory.

In short, while learning Git, only push when the target is a bare
repository; otherwise pull.

3.5. Forking a project

Sick of the way a project is being run? Think you could do a better
job? Then on your server:

```
$ git clone git://main.server/path/to/files
```

Next, tell everyone about your fork of the project at your server.

At any later time, you can merge in the changes from the original project with:

```
$ git pull
```

3.6. Ultimate backups

Want numerous tamper-proof geographically diverse redundant archives? If your project has many developers, don't do anything! Every clone of your code is effectively a backup. Not just of the current state, but of your project's entire history. Thanks to cryptographic hashing, if anyone's clone becomes corrupted, it will be spotted as soon as they try to communicate with others.

If your project is not so popular, find as many servers as you can to host clones.

The truly paranoid should always write down the latest 20-byte SHA1 hash of the HEAD somewhere safe. It has to be safe, not private. For example, publishing it in a newspaper would work well, because it's hard for an attacker to alter every copy of a newspaper.

3.7. Multitasking

Say you want to work on several features in parallel. Then commit your project and run:

```
$ git clone . /some/new/directory
```

Git exploits hard links and file sharing as much as safely possible to create this clone, so it will be ready in a flash, and you can now work on two independent features simultaneously. For example, you can edit one clone while the other is compiling.

At any time, you can commit and pull changes from the other clone.

```
$ git pull /the/other/clone HEAD
```

3.8. Guerilla version control

Are you working on a project that uses some other version control system, and you sorely miss Git? Then initialize a Git repository in your working directory:

```
$ git init
$ git add .
$ git commit -m "Initial commit"
```

then clone it:

```
$ git clone . /some/new/directory
```

Now go to the new directory and work here instead, using Git to your heart's content. Once in a while, you'll want to sync with everyone else, in which case go to the original directory, sync using the other version control system, and type:

```
$ git add .
$ git commit -m "Sync with everyone else"
```

Then go to the new directory and run:

```
$ git commit -a -m "Description of my changes"
$ git pull
```

The procedure for giving your changes to everyone else depends on the other version control system. The new directory contains the files with your changes. Run whatever commands of the other version control system are needed to upload them to the central repository.

Subversion, perhaps the best centralized version control system, is used by countless projects. The **git svn** command automates the above for Subversion repositories.

3.9. Mercurial

Mercurial is a similar version control system that can almost seamlessly work in tandem with Git. With the `hg-git` plugin, a Mercurial user can losslessly push to and pull from a Git repository.

Obtain the `hg-git` plugin with Git:

```
$ git clone git://github.com/schacon/hg-git.git
```

or Mercurial:

```
$ hg clone http://bitbucket.org/durin42/hg-git/
```

Sadly, I am unaware of an analogous plugin for Git. For this reason, I advocate Git over Mercurial for the main repository, even if you prefer Mercurial. With a Mercurial project, usually a volunteer maintains a parallel Git repository to accommodate Git users, whereas thanks to the `hg-git` plugin, a Git project automatically accommodates Mercurial users.

Although the plugin can convert a Mercurial repository to a Git repository by pushing to an empty repository, this job is easier with the `hg-fast-export.sh` script, available from:

```
$ git clone git://repo.or.cz/fast-export.git
```

To convert, in an empty directory:

```
$ git init
$ hg-fast-export.sh -r /hg/repo
```

after adding the script to your `$PATH`.

3.10. Bazaar

We briefly mention Bazaar because it is the most popular free distributed version control system after Git and Mercurial.

Bazaar has the advantage of hindsight, as it is relatively young; its designers could learn from mistakes of the past, and sidestep minor historical warts. Additionally, its developers are mindful of portability and interoperation with other version control systems.

A `bzr-git` plugin lets Bazaar users work with Git repositories to some extent. The `tailor` program converts Bazaar repositories to

Git repositories, and can do so incrementally, while `bzr-fast-export` is well-suited for one-shot conversions.

3.11. Why I use Git

I originally chose Git because I heard it could manage the unimaginably unmanageable Linux kernel source. I've never felt a need to switch. Git has served admirably, and I've yet to be bitten by its flaws. As I primarily use Linux, issues on other platforms are of no concern.

Also, I prefer C programs and bash scripts to executables such as Python scripts: there are fewer dependencies, and I'm addicted to fast running times.

I did think about how Git could be improved, going so far as to write my own Git-like tool, but only as an academic exercise. Had I completed my project, I would have stayed with Git anyway, as the gains are too slight to justify using an oddball system.

Naturally, your needs and wants likely differ, and you may be better off with another system. Nonetheless, you can't go far wrong with Git.

Chapter 4. Branches

Instant branching and merging are the most lethal of Git's killer features.

Problem: External factors inevitably necessitate context switching. A severe bug manifests in the released version without warning. The deadline for a certain feature is moved closer. A developer whose help you need is about to leave. In all cases, you must abruptly drop what you are doing and focus on a completely different task.

Interrupting your train of thought can be detrimental to your productivity, and the more cumbersome it is to switch contexts, the greater the loss. With centralized version control we must download a fresh working copy from the central server. Distributed systems fare better, as we can clone the desired version locally.

But cloning still entails copying the whole working directory as well as the entire history up to the given point. Even though Git reduces the cost of this with file sharing and hard links, the project files themselves must be recreated in their entirety in the new working directory.

Solution: Git has a better tool for these situations that is much faster and more space-efficient than cloning: **git branch**.

With this magic word, the files in your directory suddenly shapeshift from one version to another. This transformation can do more than merely go back or forward in history. Your files can morph from the last release to the experimental version to the current development version to your friend's version and so on.

4.1. My first branch

Ever played one of those games where at the push of a button ("the boss key"), the screen would instantly display a spreadsheet or something? So if the boss walked in the office while you were playing the game you could quickly hide it away?

In some directory:

```
$ echo "I'm smarter than my boss" > myfile.txt
$ git init
$ git add .
$ git commit -m "Initial commit"
```

We have created a Git repository that tracks one text file containing a certain message. Now type:

```
$ git checkout -b boss
$ echo "My boss is smarter than me" > myfile.txt
$ git commit -a -m "Another commit"
```

It looks like we've just overwritten our file and committed it. But it's an illusion. Type:

```
$ git checkout master
```

and hey presto! The text file is restored. And if the boss decides to snoop around this directory, type:

```
$ git checkout boss
```

You can switch between the two versions of the file as much as you like, and commit to each independently.

4.2. Dirty work

Say you're working on some feature, and for some reason, you need to go back three versions and temporarily put in a few print statements to see how something works. Then:

```
$ git commit -a
$ git checkout HEAD~3
```

Now you can add ugly temporary code all over the place. You can even commit these changes. When you're done,

```
$ git checkout master
```

to return to your original work. Observe that any uncommitted changes are carried over.

What if you wanted to save the temporary changes after all? Easy:

```
$ git checkout -b dirty
```

and commit before switching back to the master branch. Whenever you want to return to the dirty changes, simply type

```
$ git checkout dirty
```

We touched upon this command in an earlier chapter, when discussing loading old states. At last we can tell the whole story: the files change to the requested state, but we must leave the master branch. Any commits made from now on take your files down a different road, which can be named later.

In other words, after checking out an old state, Git automatically puts you in a new, unnamed branch, which can be named and saved with **git checkout -b**.

4.3. Quick fixes

You're in the middle of something when you are told to drop everything and fix a newly discovered bug in commit `1b6d...`:

```
$ git commit -a
$ git checkout -b fixes 1b6d
```

Then once you've fixed the bug:

```
$ git commit -a -m "Bug fixed"
$ git push  # to the central repository
$ git checkout master
```

and resume work on your original task.

You can even *merge* in the bugfix you just made, either by typing:

```
$ git merge fixes
```

or:

```
$ git pull
```

since you have already pushed the bugfix to the main repository.

4.4. Merging

With some version control systems, creating branches is easy but merging them back together is tough. With Git, merging is so trivial that you might be unaware of it happening.

Indeed, though we have just introduced **git merge**, we encountered merging long ago. The **pull** command in fact fetches commits and then merges them into your current branch. If you have no local changes, then the merge is a *fast forward*, a degenerate case akin to fetching the latest version in a centralized version control system. But if you do have local changes, Git will automatically merge, and report any conflicts.

Ordinarily, a commit has exactly one *parent commit*, namely, the previous commit. Merging branches together produces a commit with at least two parents. This begs the question: what commit does HEAD~10 really refer to? A commit could have multiple parents, so which one do we follow?

It turns out this notation chooses the first parent every time. This is desirable because commits in the current branch become the first parents during a merge; frequently you're only concerned with the changes you made in the current branch, as opposed to changes merged in from other branches.

You can refer to a specific parent with a caret. For example, to show the logs from the second parent:

```
$ git log HEAD^2
```

You may omit the number for the first parent. For example, to show the differences with the first parent:

```
$ git diff HEAD^
```

You can combine this notation with other types. For example:

```
$ git checkout 1b6d^^2~10 -b ancient
```

starts a new branch "ancient" representing the state 10 commits back from the second parent of the first parent of the commit starting with 1b6d.

4.5. Uninterrupted workflow

Often in hardware projects, the second step of a plan must await the completion of the first step. A car undergoing repairs might sit idly in a garage until a particular part arrives from the factory. A prototype might wait for a chip to be fabricated before construction can continue.

Software projects can be similar. The second part of a new feature may have to wait until the first part has been released and tested. Some projects require your code to be reviewed before accepting it, so you might wait until the first part is approved before starting the second part.

Thanks to painless branching and merging, we can bend the rules and work on Part II before Part I is officially ready. Suppose you have committed Part I and sent it for review. Let's say you're in the master branch. Then branch off:

```
$ git checkout -b part2
```

Next, work on Part II, committing your changes along the way. To err is human, and often you'll want to go back and fix something in Part I. If you're lucky, or very good, you can skip these lines.

```
$ git checkout master   # Go back to Part I.
$ edit files            # Fix Part I.
$ git checkout part2    # Go back to Part II.
$ git merge master      # Merge in those fixes.
```

Eventually, Part I is approved:

```
$ git checkout master   # Go back to Part I.
$ submit files          # Release to the world!
```

```
$ git merge part2        # Merge in Part II.
$ git branch -d part2
```

Now you're in the `master` branch again, with Part II in the working directory.

It's easy to extend this trick for any number of parts. It's also easy to branch off retroactively: suppose you belatedly realize you should have created a branch 7 commits ago. Then type:

```
$ git branch -m master part2
$   # Rename "master" branch to "part2".
$ git checkout HEAD~7 -b master
```

The `master` branch now contains just Part I, and the `part2` branch contains the rest.

4.6. Reorganizing a medley

Perhaps you like to work on all aspects of a project in the same branch. You want to keep works-in-progress to yourself and want others to see your commits only when they have been neatly organized. Start a couple of branches:

```
$ git checkout -b sanitized
$ git checkout -b medley
```

Next, work on anything: fix bugs, add features, add temporary code, and so forth, committing often along the way. Then:

```
$ git checkout sanitized
$ git cherry-pick medley^^
```

applies the grandparent of the head commit of the "medley" branch to the "sanitized" branch. With appropriate cherry-picks you can construct a branch that contains only permanent code, and has related commits grouped together.

4.7. Managing branches

List all branches by typing:

```
$ git branch
```

By default, you start in a branch named "master". Some advocate leaving the "master" branch untouched and creating new branches for your own edits.

The **-d** and **-m** options allow you to delete and move (rename) branches. See **git help branch**.

The "master" branch is a useful custom. Others may assume that your repository has a branch with this name, and that it contains the official version of your project. Although you can rename or obliterate the "master" branch, you might as well respect this convention.

4.8. Temporary branches

After a while you may realize you are creating short-lived branches frequently for similar reasons: every other branch merely serves to save the current state so you can briefly hop back to an older state to fix a high-priority bug or something.

It's analogous to changing the TV channel temporarily to see what else is on. But instead of pushing a couple of buttons, you have to create, check out, merge, and delete temporary branches. Luckily, Git has a shortcut that is as convenient as a TV remote control:

```
$ git stash
```

This saves the current state in a temporary location (a *stash*) and restores the previous state. Your working directory appears exactly as it was before you started editing, and you can fix bugs, pull in upstream changes, and so on. When you want to go back to the stashed state, type:

```
$ git stash apply  # May need to resolve conflicts.
```

You can have multiple stashes, and manipulate them in various ways. See **git help stash**. As you may have guessed, Git maintains branches behind the scenes to perform this magic trick.

4.9. Work how you want

You might wonder if branches are worth the bother. After all, clones are almost as fast, and you can switch between them with **cd** instead of esoteric Git commands.

Consider web browsers. Why support multiple tabs as well as multiple windows? Because allowing both accommodates a wide variety of styles. Some users like to keep only one browser window open, and use tabs for multiple webpages. Others might insist on the other extreme: multiple windows with no extra tabs anywhere. Others still prefer something in between.

Branching is like tabs for your working directory, and cloning is like opening a new browser window. These operations are fast and local, so why not experiment to find the combination that best suits you? Git lets you work exactly how you want.

Chapter 5. History

A consequence of Git's distributed nature is that history can be edited easily. But if you tamper with the past, take care: only rewrite that part of history which you alone possess. Just as nations forever argue over who committed what atrocity, if someone else has a clone whose version of history differs to yours, you will have trouble reconciling when your trees interact.

Some developers strongly feel history should be immutable, warts and all. Others feel trees should be made presentable before they are unleashed in public. Git accommodates both viewpoints. Like cloning, branching and merging, rewriting history is simply another power Git gives you. It is up to you to use it wisely.

5.1. Fixing the last commit

Did you just commit, but wish you had typed a different message? Then run:

```
$ git commit --amend
```

to change the last message. Realized you forgot to add a file? Run **git add** to add it, and then run the above command.

Want to include a few more edits in that last commit? Then make those edits and run:

```
$ git commit --amend -a
```

5.2. Fixing several commits

Let's suppose the previous problem is ten times worse. After a lengthy session you've made a bunch of commits. But you're not quite happy with the way they're organized, and some of those commit messages could use rewording. Then type:

```
$ git rebase -i HEAD~10
```

and the last 10 commits will appear in your favourite $EDITOR. A sample excerpt:

```
pick 5c6eb73 Added repo.or.cz link
pick a311a64 Reordered analogies in "Work How You Want"
pick 100834f Added push target to Makefile
```

Then:

- Remove commits by deleting lines.

- Reorder commits by reordering lines.

- Replace `pick` with:

  - `edit` to mark a commit for amending.

  - `reword` to change the log message.

  - `squash` to merge a commit with the previous one.

  - `fixup` to merge a commit with the previous one and discard the log message.

Save and quit. If you marked a commit for editing, then run:

```
$ git commit --amend
```

Otherwise, run:

```
$ git rebase --continue
```

So commit early and commit often: you can tidy up later with rebase.

5.3. Untangling local from upstream

You're working on an active project. You make some local commits over time, and then you sync with the official tree with a merge. This cycle repeats itself a few times before you're ready to push to the central tree.

But now the history in your local Git clone is a messy jumble of your changes and the official changes. You'd prefer to see all your changes in one contiguous section, and after all the upstream commits.

This is a job for **git rebase** as described above. In many cases you can use the **--onto** flag and avoid interaction.

Also see **git help rebase** for detailed examples of this amazing command. You can split commits. You can even rearrange branches of a tree.

5.4. Rewriting history

Occasionally, you need the source control equivalent of airbrushing people out of official photos, erasing them from history in a Stalinesque fashion. For example, suppose we intend to release a project, but it involves a file that should be kept private for some reason. Perhaps I left my credit card number in a text file and accidentally added it to the project. Deleting the file is insufficient, for the file can be accessed from older commits. We must remove the file from all commits:

```
$ git filter-branch --tree-filter 'rm secret/file' HEAD
```

See **git help filter-branch**, which discusses this example and gives a faster method. In general, **filter-branch** lets you alter large sections of history with a single command.

Afterwards, the `.git/refs/original` directory describes the state of affairs before the operation. Check the filter-branch command did what you wanted, then delete this directory if you wish to run more filter-branch commands.

Lastly, replace clones of your project with your revised version if you want to interact with them later.

5.5. Making history

Want to migrate a project to Git? If it's managed with one of the more well-known systems, then chances are someone has already written a script to export the whole history to Git.

Otherwise, look up **git fast-import**, which reads text input in a specific format to create Git history from scratch. Typically a script using this command is hastily cobbled together and run once, migrating the project in a single shot.

As an example, paste the following listing into temporary file, such as `/tmp/history`:

```
commit refs/heads/master
committer Alice <alice@example.com> Thu, 01 Jan 1970 00:00:00 +0000
data <<EOT
Initial commit.
EOT

M 100644 inline hello.c
data <<EOT
#include <stdio.h>

int main() {
  printf("Hello, world!\n");
  return 0;
}
EOT


commit refs/heads/master
committer Bob <bob@example.com> Tue, 14 Mar 2000 01:59:26 -0800
data <<EOT
Replace printf() with write().
EOT

M 100644 inline hello.c
data <<EOT
#include <unistd.h>

int main() {
  write(1, "Hello, world!\n", 14);
  return 0;
}
EOT
```

Then create a Git repository from this temporary file by typing:

```
$ mkdir project; cd project; git init
$ git fast-import --date-format=rfc2822 < /tmp/history
```

You can checkout the latest version of the project with:

```
$ git checkout master .
```

The **git fast-export** command converts any repository to the **git fast-import** format, whose output you can study for writing exporters, and also to transport repositories in a human-readable format. Indeed, these commands can send repositories of text files over text-only channels.

5.6. Where did it all go wrong?

You've just discovered a broken feature in your program which you know for sure was working a few months ago. Argh! Where did this bug come from? If only you had been testing the feature as you developed.

It's too late for that now. However, provided you've been committing often, Git can pinpoint the problem:

```
$ git bisect start
$ git bisect bad HEAD
$ git bisect good 1b6d
```

Git checks out a state halfway in between. Test the feature, and if it's still broken:

```
$ git bisect bad
```

If not, replace "bad" with "good". Git again transports you to a state halfway between the known good and bad versions, narrowing down the possibilities. After a few iterations, this binary search will lead you to the commit that caused the trouble. Once you've finished your investigation, return to your original state by typing:

```
$ git bisect reset
```

Instead of testing every change by hand, automate the search by running:

```
$ git bisect run my_script
```

Git uses the return value of the given command, typically a one-off script, to decide whether a change is good or bad: the command should exit with code 0 when good, 125 when the change should be skipped, and anything else between 1 and 127 if it is bad. A negative return value aborts the bisect.

You can do much more: the help page explains how to visualize bisects, examine or replay the bisect log, and eliminate known innocent changes for a speedier search.

5.7. Who's to blame?

Like many other version control systems, Git has a blame command:

```
$ git blame bug.c
```

which annotates every line in the given file showing who last changed it, and when. Unlike many other version control systems, this operation works offline, reading only from local disk.

5.8. Personal experience

In a centralized version control system, history modification is a difficult operation, and only available to administrators. Cloning, branching, and merging are impossible without network communication. So are basic operations such as browsing history, or committing a change. In some systems, users require network connectivity just to view their own changes or open a file for editing.

Centralized systems preclude working offline, and need more expensive network infrastructure, especially as the number of developers grows. Most importantly, all operations are slower to some degree, usually to the point where users shun advanced commands unless absolutely necessary. In extreme cases this is true of even the most basic commands. When users must run slow commands, productivity suffers because of an interrupted work flow.

I experienced these phenomena first-hand. Git was the first version control system I used. I quickly grew accustomed to it, taking many features for granted. I simply assumed other systems were similar: choosing a version control system ought to be no different from choosing a text editor or web browser.

I was shocked when later forced to use a centralized system. A flaky internet connection matters little with Git, but makes development unbearable when it needs to be as reliable as local disk. Additionally, I found myself conditioned to avoid certain commands because of the latencies involved, which ultimately prevented me from following my desired work flow.

When I had to run a slow command, the interruption to my train of thought dealt a disproportionate amount of damage. While waiting for server communication to complete, I'd do something else to pass the time, such as check email or write documentation. By the time I returned to the original task, the command had finished long ago, and I would waste more time trying to remember what I was doing. Humans are bad at context switching.

There was also an interesting tragedy-of-the-commons effect: anticipating network congestion, individuals would consume more bandwidth than necessary on various operations in an attempt to reduce future delays. The combined efforts intensified congestion, encouraging individuals to consume even more bandwidth next time to avoid even longer delays.

Chapter 6. Social version control

Initially I used Git on a private project where I was the sole developer. Amongst the commands related to Git's distributed nature, I needed only **pull** and **clone** so could I keep the same project in different places.

Later I wanted to publish my code with Git, and include changes from contributors. I had to learn how to manage projects with multiple developers from all over the world. Fortunately, this is Git's forte, and arguably its raison d'être.

6.1. Who am I?

Every commit has an author name and email, which is shown by **git log**. By default, Git uses system settings to populate these fields. To set them explicitly, type:

```
$ git config --global user.name "John Doe"
$ git config --global user.email johndoe@example.com
```

Omit the global flag to set these options only for the current repository.

6.2. Git over SSH, HTTP

Suppose you have SSH access to a web server, but Git is not installed. Though less efficient than its native protocol, Git can communicate over HTTP.

Download, compile and install Git in your account, and create a repository in your web directory:

```
$ GIT_DIR=proj.git git init
$ cd proj.git
$ git --bare update-server-info
$ cp hooks/post-update.sample hooks/post-update
```

For older versions of Git, instead of the copy command, run:

```
$ chmod a+x hooks/post-update
```

Now you can publish your latest edits via SSH from any clone:

```
$ git push web.server:/path/to/proj.git master
```

and anybody can get your project with:

```
$ git clone http://web.server/proj.git
```

6.3. Git over anything

Want to synchronize repositories without servers, or even a network connection? Need to improvise during an emergency? We've seen **git fast-export** and **git fast-import** can convert repositories to a single file and back. We could shuttle such files back and forth to transport git repositories over any medium, but a more efficient tool is **git bundle**.

The sender creates a *bundle*:

```
$ git bundle create somefile HEAD
```

then transports the bundle, `somefile`, to the other party somehow: email, thumb drive, an **xxd** printout and an OCR scanner, reading bits over the phone, smoke signals, etc. The receiver retrieves commits from the bundle by typing:

```
$ git pull somefile
```

The receiver can even do this from an empty repository. Despite its size, `somefile` contains the entire original git repository.

In larger projects, eliminate waste by bundling only changes the other repository lacks. For example, suppose the commit "1b6d..." is the most recent commit shared by both parties:

```
$ git bundle create somefile HEAD ^1b6d
```

If done frequently, one could easily forget which commit was last sent. The help page suggests using tags to solve this. Namely, after you send a bundle, type:

```
$ git tag -f lastbundle HEAD
```

and create new refresher bundles with:

```
$ git bundle create newbundle HEAD ^lastbundle
```

6.4. Patches

Patches are text representations of your changes that can be easily understood by computers and humans alike. This gives them universal appeal. You can email a patch to developers no matter what version control system they're using. As long as your audience can read their email, they can see your edits. Similarly, on your side, all you require is an email account: there's no need to setup an online Git repository.

Recall from the first chapter:

```
$ git diff 1b6d > my.patch
```

outputs a patch which can be pasted into an email for discussion. In a Git repository, type:

```
$ git apply < my.patch
```

to apply the patch.

In more formal settings, when author names and perhaps signatures should be recorded, generate the corresponding patches past a certain point by typing:

```
$ git format-patch 1b6d
```

The resulting files can be given to **git-send-email**, or sent by hand. You can also specify a range of commits:

```
$ git format-patch 1b6d..HEAD^^
```

On the receiving end, save an email to a file, then type:

```
$ git am < email.txt
```

This applies the incoming patch and also creates a commit, including information such as the author.

With a browser email client, you may need to click a button to see the email in its raw original form before saving the patch to a file.

There are slight differences for mbox-based email clients, but if you use one of these, you're probably the sort of person who can figure them out easily without reading tutorials!

6.5. Sorry, we've moved

After cloning a repository, running **git push** or **git pull** will automatically push to or pull from the original URL. How does Git do this? The secret lies in config options created with the clone. Let's take a peek:

```
$ git config --list
```

The `remote.origin.url` option controls the source URL; "origin" is a nickname given to the source repository. As with the "master" branch convention, we may change or delete this nickname but there is usually no reason for doing so.

If the original repository moves, we can update the URL via:

```
$ git config remote.origin.url git://new.url/proj.git
```

The `branch.master.merge` option specifies the default remote branch in a **git pull**. During the initial clone, it is set to the current branch of the source repository, so even if the HEAD of the source repository subsequently moves to a different branch, a later pull will faithfully follow the original branch.

This option only applies to the repository we first cloned from, which is recorded in the option `branch.master.remote`. If we pull in from other repositories we must explicitly state which branch we want:

```
$ git pull git://example.com/other.git master
```

The above explains why some of our earlier push and pull examples had no arguments.

6.6. Remote branches

When you clone a repository, you also clone all its branches. You may not have noticed this because Git hides them away: you must ask for them specifically. This prevents branches in the remote repository from interfering with your branches, and also makes Git easier for beginners.

List the remote branches with:

```
$ git branch -r
```

You should see something like:

```
origin/HEAD
origin/master
origin/experimental
```

These represent branches and the HEAD of the remote repository, and can be used in regular Git commands. For example, suppose you have made many commits, and wish to compare against the last fetched version. You could search through the logs for the appropriate SHA1 hash, but it's much easier to type:

```
$ git diff origin/HEAD
```

Or you can see what the "experimental" branch has been up to:

```
$ git log origin/experimental
```

6.7. Multiple remotes

Suppose two other developers are working on our project, and we want to keep tabs on both. We can follow more than one repository at a time with:

```
$ git remote add other git://example.com/some_repo.git
$ git pull other some_branch
```

Now we have merged in a branch from the second repository, and we have easy access to all branches of all repositories:

```
$ git diff origin/experimental^ other/some_branch~5
```

But what if we just want to compare their changes without affecting our own work? In other words, we want to examine their branches without having their changes invade our working directory. Then rather than pull, run:

```
$ git fetch         # Fetch from origin, the default.
$ git fetch other   # Fetch from the second programmer.
```

This just fetches histories. Although the working directory remains untouched, we can refer to any branch of any repository in a Git command because we now possess a local copy.

Recall that behind the scenes, a pull is simply a **fetch** then **merge**. Usually we **pull** because we want to merge the latest commit after a fetch; this situation is a notable exception.

See **git help remote** for how to remove remote repositories, ignore certain branches, and more.

6.8. My preferences

For my projects, I like contributors to prepare repositories from which I can pull. Some Git hosting services let you host your own fork of a project with the click of a button.

After I fetch a tree, I run Git commands to navigate and examine the changes, which ideally are well-organized and well-described. I merge my own changes, and perhaps make further edits. Once satisfied, I push to the main repository.

Staying in the Git world is slightly more convenient than patch files, as it saves me from converting them to Git commits. Furthermore, Git handles details such as recording the author's name and email address, as well as the time and date, and asks the author to describe their own change.

Chapter 7. Git grandmastery

By now, you should be able to navigate the **git help** pages and
understand almost everything. However, pinpointing the exact
command required to solve a given problem can be tedious. Perhaps
I can save you some time: below are some recipes I have needed in
the past.

7.1. Archiving projects

For my projects, Git tracks exactly the files I'd like to archive and
release to users. To create a tarball of the source code, I run:

```
$ git archive --format=tar --prefix=proj-1.2.3/ HEAD
```

7.2. Commit what changed

Telling Git when you've added, deleted and renamed files is
troublesome for certain projects. Instead, you can type:

```
$ git add .
$ git add -u
```

Git will look at the files in the current directory and work out the
details by itself. Instead of the second add command, run `git
commit -a` if you also intend to commit at this time. See **git help
ignore** for how to specify files that should be ignored.

You can perform the above in a single pass with:

```
$ git ls-files -dmo -z \
  | xargs -0 git update-index --add --remove
```

The **-z** and **-0** options prevent ill side-effects from filenames
containing strange characters. As this command adds ignored files,
you may want to use the `-x` or `-X` option.

7.3. My commit is too big!

Have you neglected to commit for too long? Been coding furiously
and forgotten about source control until now? Made a series of
unrelated changes, because that's your style?

No worries. Run:

```
$ git add -p
```

For each edit you made, Git will show you the hunk of code that was changed, and ask if it should be part of the next commit. Answer with "y" or "n". You have other options, such as postponing the decision; type "?" to learn more.

Once you're satisfied, type

```
$ git commit
```

to commit precisely the changes you selected (the *staged* changes). Make sure you omit the **-a** option, otherwise Git will commit all the edits.

What if you've edited many files in many places? Reviewing each change one by one becomes frustratingly mind-numbing. In this case, use **git add -i**, whose interface is less straightforward, but more flexible. With a few keystrokes, you can stage or unstage several files at a time, or review and select changes in particular files only. Alternatively, run **git commit --interactive** which automatically commits after you're done.

7.4. The index: Git's staging area

So far we have avoided Git's famous *index*, but we must now confront it to explain the above. The index is a temporary staging area. Git seldom shuttles data directly between your project and its history. Rather, Git first writes data to the index, and then copies the data in the index to its final destination.

For example, **commit -a** is really a two-step process. The first step places a snapshot of the current state of every tracked file into the index. The second step permanently records the snapshot now in the index. Committing without the **-a** option only performs the second step, and only makes sense after running commands that somehow change the index, such as **git add**.

Usually we can ignore the index and pretend we are reading straight from and writing straight to the history. On this occasion, we want finer control, so we manipulate the index. We place a snapshot of some, but not all, of our changes into the index, and then permanently record this carefully rigged snapshot.

7.5. Lost your HEAD?

Recall the HEAD tag normally points at the latest commit. Some Git commands let you move it. For example:

```
$ git reset HEAD~3
```

will move the HEAD three commits back. Thus all Git commands now act as if you hadn't made those last three commits, while your files remain in the present. See the help page for some applications.

But how can you go back to the future? The past commits know nothing of the future.

If you have the SHA1 of the original HEAD then:

```
$ git reset 1b6d
```

But suppose you never took it down? Don't worry: for commands like these, Git saves the original HEAD as a tag called ORIG_HEAD, and you can return safe and sound with:

```
$ git reset ORIG_HEAD
```

7.6. HEAD-hunting

Perhaps ORIG_HEAD isn't enough. Perhaps you've just realized you made a monumental mistake and you need to go back to an ancient commit in a long-forgotten branch.

By default, Git keeps a commit for at least two weeks, even if you ordered Git to destroy the branch containing it. The trouble is finding the appropriate hash. You could look at all the hash values in .git/objects and use trial and error to find the one you want. But there's a much easier way.

Git records every hash of a commit it computes in `.git/logs`. The subdirectory `refs` contains the history of all activity on all branches, while the file `HEAD` shows every hash value it has ever taken. The latter can be used to find hashes of commits on branches that have been accidentally lopped off.

The reflog command provides a friendly interface to these log files. Try

```
$ git reflog
```

Instead of cutting and pasting hashes from the reflog, try:

```
$ git checkout "@{10 minutes ago}"
```

Or checkout the 5th-last visited commit via:

```
$ git checkout "@{5}"
```

See the "Specifying Revisions" section of **git help rev-parse** for more.

You may wish to configure a longer grace period for doomed commits. For example:

```
$ git config gc.pruneexpire "30 days"
```

means a deleted commit will only be permanently lost once 30 days have passed and **git gc** is run.

You may also wish to disable automatic invocations of **git gc**:

```
$ git config gc.auto 0
```

in which case commits will only be deleted when you run **git gc** manually.

7.7. Building on Git

In true UNIX fashion, Git's design allows it to be easily used as a low-level component of other programs, such as GUI and web interfaces, alternative command-line interfaces, patch managements tools, importing and conversion tools and so on. In fact, some Git commands are themselves scripts standing on the shoulders of giants. With a little tinkering, you can customize Git to suit your preferences.

One easy trick is to use built-in Git aliases to shorten your most frequently used commands:

```
$ git config --global alias.co checkout
$   # display current aliases
$ git config --global --get-regexp alias
alias.co checkout
$ git co foo  # same as 'git checkout foo'
```

One easy trick is to use built-in Git aliases to shorten your most frequently Another is to print the current branch in the prompt, or window title. Invoking

```
$ git symbolic-ref HEAD
```

shows the current branch name. In practice, you most likely want to remove the "refs/heads/" and ignore errors:

```
$ git symbolic-ref HEAD 2> /dev/null | cut -b 12-
```

The `contrib` subdirectory is a treasure trove of tools built on Git. In time, some of them may be promoted to official commands. On Debian and Ubuntu, this directory lives at `/usr/share/doc/git-core/contrib`.

One popular resident is `workdir/git-new-workdir`. Via clever symlinking, this script creates a new working directory whose history is shared with the original repository:

```
$ git-new-workdir an/existing/repo new/directory
```

The new directory and the files within can be thought of as a clone, except since the history is shared, the two trees automatically stay in sync. There's no need to merge, push or pull.

7.8. Overriding safeguards

These days, Git makes it difficult for the user to accidentally destroy data. But if you know what you are doing, you can destroy data on purpose.

Checkout: Uncommitted changes cause checkout to fail. To destroy your changes, and checkout a given commit anyway, use the force flag:

```
$ git checkout -f HEAD^
```

On the other hand, if you specify particular paths for checkout, then there are no safety checks. The supplied paths are quietly overwritten. Take care if you use checkout in this manner.

Reset: Reset also fails in the presence of uncommitted changes. To force it through, run:

```
$ git reset --hard 1b6d
```

Branch: Deleting branches fails if this causes changes to be lost. To force a deletion, type:

```
$ git branch -D dead_branch  # instead of -d
```

Similarly, attempting to overwrite a branch via a move fails if data loss would ensue. To force a branch move, type:

```
$ git branch -M source target  # instead of -m
```

Unlike checkout and reset, these two commands defer data destruction. The changes are still stored in the .git subdirectory, and can be retrieved by recovering the appropriate hash from `.git/logs` (see "HEAD-hunting" above). By default, they will be kept for at least two weeks.

Clean: Some git commands refuse to proceed because they're worried about clobbering untracked files. If you're certain that all untracked files and directories are expendable, then delete them mercilessly with:

```
$ git clean -f -d
```

Next time, that pesky command will work!

7.9. Preventing bad commits

Stupid mistakes abound in the histories of many of my projects.
The most frightening are missing files due to a forgotten **git add**.
Luckily I have yet to lose crucial data though accidental omission
because I rarely delete original working directories. I typically
notice the error a few commits later, so the only damage is a bit of
missing history and a sheepish admission of guilt.

I also regularly commit (literally and git-erally) the lesser
transgression of trailing whitespace. Though harmless, I wish these
also never appeared on the public record.

In addition, though unscathed so far, I worry about leaving merge
conflicts unresolved. Usually I catch them when I build a project,
but this can miss some cases.

If only I had bought idiot insurance by using a *hook* to alert me
about these problems:

```
$ cd .git/hooks
$ cp pre-commit.sample pre-commit
```

Now Git aborts a commit if useless whitespace or unresolved merge
conflicts are detected.

For this guide, I eventually added the following to the beginning of
the **pre-commit** hook to guard against absent-mindedness:

```
if git ls-files -o | grep '\.txt$'; then
  echo FAIL! Untracked .txt files.
  exit 1
fi
```

Several git operations support hooks; see **git help hooks**. One
can write hooks to complain about spelling mistakes in commit

messages, add new files, indent paragraphs, append an entry to a webpage, play a sound, and so on.

We activated the sample **post-update** hook earlier when discussing Git over HTTP; this causes Git to run this script whenever the head has moved. The sample post-update script updates a few files Git needs for communication over Git-agnostic transports such as HTTP.

Chapter 8. How Git works

We take a peek under the hood and explain how Git performs its
miracles. It's akin to learning how a skilled conjurer performs a
mind-blowing magic trick: on the one hand, the secrets are almost
disappointingly straightforward, but on the other hand, you are in
awe that so much can be achieved with so little.

8.1. Invisibility

How can Git be so unobtrusive? Aside from occasional commits and
merges, you can work as if you were unaware that version control
exists. That is, until you need it, and that's when you're glad Git
was watching over you the whole time.

Other version control systems force you to constantly struggle with
red tape and bureaucracy. Permissions of files may be read-only
unless you explicitly tell a central server which files you intend to
edit. The most basic commands may slow to a crawl as the number
of users increases. Work grinds to a halt when the network or the
central server goes down.

In contrast, Git simply keeps the history of your project in the `.git`
directory in your working directory. This is your own copy of the
history, so you can stay offline until you want to communicate with
others. You have total control over the fate of your files because Git
can easily recreate a saved state from `.git` at any time.

8.2. Integrity

Most people associate cryptography with keeping information
secret, but another equally important goal is keeping information
safe. Proper use of cryptographic hash functions can prevent
accidental or malicious data corruption.

A SHA1 hash can be thought of as a unique 160-bit ID number for
every string of bytes you'll encounter in your life. Actually more
than that: every string of bytes that any human will ever use over
many lifetimes.

As a SHA1 hash is itself a string of bytes, we can hash strings of bytes containing other hashes. This simple observation is surprisingly useful: look up *hash chains*. We'll later see how Git uses it to efficiently guarantee data integrity.

Briefly, Git keeps your data in the `.git/objects` subdirectory, where instead of normal filenames, you'll find only IDs. By using IDs as filenames, as well as a few lockfiles and timestamping tricks, Git transforms any humble filesystem into an efficient and robust database.

8.3. Rename detection

How does Git know you renamed a file, even though you never mentioned the fact explicitly? Sure, you may have run **git mv**, but that is exactly the same as a **git rm** followed by a **git add**.

Git heuristically ferrets out renames and copies between successive versions. In fact, it can detect chunks of code being moved or copied around between files! Though it cannot cover all cases, it does a decent job, and this feature is always improving. If it fails to work for you, try options enabling more expensive copy detection, and consider upgrading.

8.4. The index

 For every tracked file, Git records information such as its size, creation time and last modification time in a file known as the *index*. To determine whether a file has changed, Git compares its current stats with those cached in the index. If they match, then Git can skip reading the file again.

Since stat calls are considerably faster than file reads, if you only edit a few files, Git can update its state in almost no time.

We stated earlier that the index is a staging area. Then how can the index just be a bunch of file stats?

The index can be thought of as a staging area because the add command puts files into Git's database and updates the index accordingly, while the commit command, without options, creates a commit based on the state of the index.

8.5. The object database

Every version of your data is kept in the *object database*, which lives in the subdirectory .git/objects; the other residents of .git/ hold lesser data: the index, branch names, tags, configuration options, logs, the current location of the head commit, and so on. The object database is elementary yet elegant, and the source of Git's power.

Each file within .git/objects is an *object*. There are 3 kinds of objects that concern us: *blob* objects, *tree* objects, and *commit* objects.

8.6. Blobs

First, a magic trick. Pick a filename, any filename. In an empty directory:

```
$ echo sweet > FILENAME
$ git init
$ git add .
$ find .git/objects -type f
```

You'll see .git/objects/ aa/823728ea7d592acc69b36875a482cdf3fd5c8d.

How do I know this without knowing the filename? It's because the SHA1 hash of:

```
"blob" SP "6" NUL "sweet" LF
```

is aa823728ea7d592acc69b36875a482cdf3fd5c8d, where SP is a space, NUL is a zero byte and LF is a linefeed. You can verify this by typing:

```
$ printf "blob 6\000sweet\n" | sha1sum
```

Git is *content-addressable*: files are not stored according to their filename, but rather by the hash of the data they contain, in a file we call a *blob object*. We can think of the hash as a unique ID for a file's contents, so in a sense we are addressing files by their content. The initial `blob 6` is merely a header consisting of the object type and its length in bytes; it simplifies internal bookkeeping.

Thus I could easily predict what you would see. The file's name is irrelevant: only the data inside is used to construct the blob object.

You may be wondering what happens to identical files. Try adding copies of your file, with any filenames whatsoever. The contents of `.git/objects` stay the same no matter how many you add. Git only stores the data once.

By the way, the files within `.git/objects` are compressed with zlib so you should not stare at them directly. Filter them through **zpipe -d** (see the `zlib` library), or type:

```
$ git cat-file -p aa82
```

which pretty-prints the given object.

8.7. Trees

But where are the filenames? They must be stored somewhere at some stage. Git gets around to the filenames during a commit:

```
$ git commit  # Type some message.
$ find .git/objects -type f
```

You should now see 3 objects. This time I cannot tell you what the 2 new files are, as it partly depends on the filename you picked. We'll proceed assuming you chose "rose". If you didn't, you can rewrite history to make it look like you did:

```
$ git filter-branch --tree-filter 'mv FILENAME rose'
$ find .git/objects -type f
```

Now you should see the file `.git/objects/05/b217bb859794d08bb9e4f7f04cbda4b207fbe9`, because this is the SHA1 hash of its contents:

```
"tree" SP "32" NUL "100644 rose" NUL
```

```
0xaa823728ea7d592acc69b36875a482cdf3fd5c8d
```

Check this file does indeed contain the above by typing:

```
$ echo 05b217bb859794d08bb9e4f7f04cbda4b207fbe9 \
  | git cat-file --batch
```

We can verify the hash with zpipe:

```
$ zpipe -d < .git/objects/05/b2* | sha1sum
```

Hash verification is trickier via cat-file because its output contains more than the raw uncompressed object file.

This file is a *tree* object: a list of tuples consisting of a file type, a filename, and a hash. In our example, the file type is 100644, which means 'rose` is a normal file, and the hash is the blob object that contains the contents of `rose'. Other possible file types are executables, symlinks or directories. In the last case, the hash points to a tree object.

If you ran filter-branch, you'll have old objects you no longer need. Although they will be jettisoned automatically once the grace period expires, we'll delete them now to make our toy example easier to follow:

```
$ rm -r .git/refs/original
$ git reflog expire --expire=now --all
$ git prune
```

For real projects you should typically avoid commands like this, as you are destroying backups. If you want a clean repository, it is usually best to make a fresh clone. Also, take care when directly manipulating .git: what if a Git command is running at the same time, or a sudden power outage occurs? In general, refs should be deleted with **git update-ref -d**, though usually it's safe to remove refs/original by hand.

8.8. Commits

We've explained 2 of the 3 objects. The third is a *commit* object. Its contents depend on the commit message as well as the date and time it was created. To match what we have here, we'll have to tweak it a little:

```
$   # Change the commit message.
$ git commit --amend -m Shakespeare
$   # Rig timestamps and authors.
$ git filter-branch --env-filter 'export
GIT_AUTHOR_DATE="Fri 13 Feb 2009 15:31:30 -0800"
GIT_AUTHOR_NAME="Alice"
GIT_AUTHOR_EMAIL="alice@example.com"
GIT_COMMITTER_DATE="Fri, 13 Feb 2009 15:31:30 -0800"
GIT_COMMITTER_NAME="Bob"
GIT_COMMITTER_EMAIL="bob@example.com"'
$ find .git/objects -type f
```

You should now see `.git/objects/49/993fe130c4b3bf24857a15d7969c396b7bc187` which is the SHA1 hash of its contents:

```
"commit 158" NUL
"tree 05b217bb859794d08bb9e4f7f04cbda4b207fbe9" LF
"author Alice <alice@example.com> 1234567890 -0800" LF
"committer Bob <bob@example.com> 1234567890 -0800" LF
LF
"Shakespeare" LF
```

As before, you can run zpipe or cat-file to see for yourself.

This is the first commit, so there are no parent commits, but later commits will always contain at least one line identifying a parent commit.

8.9. Indistinguishable from magic

Git's secrets seem too simple. It looks like you could mix together a few shell scripts and add a dash of C code to cook it up in a matter of hours: a melange of basic filesystem operations and SHA1 hashing, garnished with lock files and fsyncs for robustness. In fact, this accurately describes the earliest versions of Git. Nonetheless, apart from ingenious packing tricks to save space, and ingenious indexing tricks to save time, we now know how Git deftly changes a filesystem into a database perfect for version control.

For example, if any file within the object database is corrupted by a disk error, then its hash will no longer match, alerting us to the problem. By hashing hashes of other objects, we maintain integrity at all levels. Commits are atomic, that is, a commit can never only partially record changes: we can only compute the hash of a commit and store it in the database after we already have stored all relevant trees, blobs and parent commits. The object database is immune to unexpected interruptions such as power outages.

We defeat even the most devious adversaries. Suppose somebody attempts to stealthily modify the contents of a file in an ancient version of a project. To keep the object database looking healthy, they must also change the hash of the corresponding blob object since it's now a different string of bytes. This means they'll have to change the hash of any tree object referencing the file, and in turn change the hash of all commit objects involving such a tree, in addition to the hashes of all the descendants of these commits. This implies the hash of the official head differs to that of the bad repository. By following the trail of mismatching hashes we can pinpoint the mutilated file, as well as the commit where it was first corrupted.

In short, so long as the 20 bytes representing the last commit are safe, it's impossible to tamper with a Git repository.

What about Git's renowned features? Branching? Merging? Tags? Mere details. The current head is kept in the file `.git/HEAD`, which contains a hash of a commit object. The hash gets updated during a commit as well as many other commands. Branches are almost the same: they are files in `.git/refs/heads`. Tags too: they live in `.git/refs/tags` but they are updated by a different set of commands.

Index

A

add command, 5
aliases, 43
am command, 35
apply command, 9, 35
archive command, 39

B

bare repository, 12
Bazaar, 16
bisect command, 30
blame command, 31
blob object, 49
branch, 18
branch command, 23
branch creation, 18
branch management, 23
bundle command, 34

C

cat-file command, 50
centralized version control, 2
checkout command, 6
cherry-pick command, 23
clean command, 44
clone, 11
clone command, 8
commit command, 5
commit object, 51
config command, 33, 43

D

daemon command, 12
diff command, 9, 35
distributed version control, 2

F

fast-import command, 29
fetch command, 38
filter-branch command, 28
format-patch command, 35

G

garbage collection, 42
gc command, 42
git-new-workdir script, 43

H

HEAD tag, 11, 41
hg-git plugin, 15
hook, 45
HTTP transport, 33

I

index, 40, 48
init command, 5
instaweb command, 10

L

log command, 6, 8
ls-files command, 39

M

Mercurial, 15
merge command, 20
merge conflict, 4
merging branches, 21
mv command, 5

O

object database, 49
ORIG_HEAD tag, 41